YOUR NAME

_____

DATE YOU'RE STARTING THIS JOURNEY

(YOU'RE GONNA COMMIT RIGHT?)

_____

Patient
WISDOM
Endless
STRENGTH
Fearless
LOVE

Welcome.

Inside this journal you'll find things to think about and exercises to do. Most of them require just a little of your time, but the quality of thought and energy you put into your answers will determine your transformation.

The journal prompts will improve your relationships all around, but more importantly, they'll improve *you.*

Some you can write in the space provided, make your own, or just meditate on the answers. But treat them with care.

Don't put them off or make the mistake of merely *thinking* about doing them. Do one each day and put your heart into it. Doing so will separate you from the other husbands, dads and men who are comfortable where they are, afraid of change.

This is your journey. One day at a time.

Go inside and be honest with yourself. Then keep this book and review your answers…you may surprise yourself at what accomplishments you've made in a few months, what relationships you've improved, and what obstacles you've overcome in all areas of your life.

Few look inside…

Fewer still work on what they see.

The time is now. Good luck…

Are you ready?

DIG
DEEP

WHY DID YOU BUY THIS JOURNAL? IT **ALL** STARTS WITH "WHY"
TAKE SOME TIME AND WRITE OUT YOUR THOUGHTS <u>BELOW</u>
THIS WILL **HELP** AND **GUIDE** YOU AS YOU **COMPLETE YOUR JOURNEY**

Bitterness rots a soul and can lead to constant anger, especially in your relationship with your wife. What can you let go of today? *Really* resolve to let go of? Write down something you said or regret doing this last week, then say, "I let it go in peace" and scribble it all out on the page.

Describe the values you want for your kids. Be clear and specific. When you're done, imagine yourself modeling those behaviors and values for your kids daily. Think about this for at least five minutes today, and work towards improving just one area at a time.

WHAT ARE SOME GOOD BOOKS YOU'VE SEEN LATELY THAT HAVE PIQUED YOUR INTEREST IN THE SELF-IMPROVEMENT AREA?

WHETHER IT'S ON FINANCE, MINDSET OR RELATIONSHIPS, PICK ONE AND SET ASIDE TWENTY MINUTES TO READ IT EACH DAY UNTIL FINISHED.

CONCENTRATE ON JUST THAT ONE BOOK, AND MAKE NOTES, OUTLINING THE STEPS TO INCORPORATE THE IDEAS INTO YOUR OWN LIFE.

Describe your dream job. Are you in it? Can you get it? If not, can you marry some of the characteristics of your dream job to the one you have now? Maybe you work from home more, or start earlier and leave sooner. Whatever it is, you can make changes that matter to your mental and spiritual health, starting this week. Write how below.

SKETCH SOMEONE YOU LOVE BELOW. HAVE FUN WITH IT. SHOW THEM
LATER IF YOU WANT.

LISTEN. REALLY *LISTEN* TO YOUR WIFE TALK ABOUT HER DAY. DON'T INTERRUPT, JUST LISTEN ACTIVELY. AND BY ACTIVELY, THAT MEANS DON'T BE THINKING ABOUT WHAT YOU'RE GOING TO SAY NEXT, OR WORSE, BE LOOKING AT YOUR PHONE. PUT EVERYTHING ASIDE AND REALLY FOCUS ON HER.

PLAY WITH YOUR KIDS.
LET THEM PICK THE GAME OR ACTIVITY. DON'T TRY TO DO IT
"YOUR STYLE" BUT LET THEM MAKE ALL THE RULES. THEN *ENJOY*
IT.

THIS IS FOR THEM

List 5 things you can do, this week, to start taking better care of your mindset. What do you need to guard it from? Your mind and heart can take direction, the question is, what are they taking direction from?

WHERE CAN YOU TAKE YOUR CHILDREN THIS WEEK

OR WEEKEND TO MAKE THEM FEEL SPECIAL.

SOMETHING THEY LOVE THAT YOU DO FOR THEM?

HOW MUCH MORE TIME COULD YOU GAIN IF YOU PUT YOUR PHONE DOWN FOR AN HOUR, LEFT YOUR WORK AT THE OFFICE INSTEAD OF LEAVING IT IN YOUR HEAD AT NIGHT, AND PAID ATTENTION TO YOUR WIFE?

IMAGINE HOW MUCH LOVE AND SUPPORT YOU'D GAIN JUST BY TURNING THOSE THINGS OFF FOR THE NIGHT. YOU WOULDN'T EVEN HAVE TO TELL HER. SHE'LL NOTICE...

BUY DONUTS AND SURPRISE YOUR KIDS WITH THEM FOR BREAKFAST TOMORROW.

IF IT'S A SCHOOL DAY, **ALL THE BETTER AND MORE SPECIAL.**

List 5 things your wife did that made you happy this week.

GO FOR A WALK OUTSIDE WITH YOUR KIDS. REALLY.

DO IT.

THEY'LL OPEN UP TO YOU AND YOU'LL BOTH ENJOY THE FRESH
AIR.

GO FOR A RUN, OR A WALK, TODAY. LIFT WEIGHTS IF YOU HAVE THEM (EVEN IF THEY'RE COLLECTING DUST IN YOUR BASEMENT). **IMPROVE YOUR HEALTH ONE DAY AT A TIME** BY DOING SOMETHING FOR TWENTY MINUTES, STARTING TODAY.

What music changes your moods and how?

Can you put that on to change your day and inspire you right now?

DO THE LAUNDRY TODAY. A COUPLE LOADS IF YOU CAN.

VACUUM IN BETWEEN LOADS. SHOW YOUR WIFE YOU CARE ABOUT THE HOUSE AS MUCH AS SHE DOES.

HOW MANY ARGUMENTS WITH YOUR WIFE COULD BE AVOIDED ALTOGETHER BY SIMPLY AVOIDING BRINGING UP OLD ISSUES FOR NO REASON? YOU DON'T HAVE TO WIN ALL THE TIME EITHER. SOMETIMES YOU WIN BY LETTING GO.

PLAY TIC-TAC-TOE WITH YOUR KIDS BELOW.
DO IT TODAY.

Plan. Write out something meaningful that you hope to accomplish today. Figure out the steps you need to take to improve your life in this one, small way and set out to make it happen no matter what. Good things happen piece by piece.

What's your SELF-TALK? Analyze your habitual thought patterns than work on catching yourself when you're negative on life and yourself. SWAP THOSE THOUGHTS FOR SOMETHING POSITIVE IMMEDIATELY, and watch your life change drastically. It works. But you have to catch and squash unproductive worry and thoughts as they arise. Practice this starting now.

TAKE YOUR WIFE'S CAR AND PUT GAS IN THE TANK, GIVE IT A WASH AND CLEAN IT OUT. SURPRISE HER, AND MAYBE EVEN LEAVE A NICE FLOWER ON THE SEAT.

LIST 6 THINGS YOUR KIDS DID THAT MADE YOU HAPPY OR PROUD THIS WEEK.

1.

2.

3.

4.

5.

6

DESCRIBE BELOW HOW YOU WANT THE WORLD TO PERCEIVE YOU? WHAT KIND OF QUALITIES DO YOU HAVE? DO OTHERS WANT TO BE LIKE YOU?

CALL YOUR MOM OR DAD. TELL THEM YOU LOVE THEM. OR
YOUR SISTER OR BROTHER. THEN LISTEN TO HOW THEIR DAY
IS GOING.

SOMEONE IN YOUR FAMILY HAS BEEN WAITING TO HEAR
FROM YOU. NOW IS THE TIME.

SCHEDULE THAT DOCTOR'S APPOINTMENT. WHETHER IT'S A PHYSICAL, TOOTH, OR EYE APPOINTMENT, **MAKE THE CALL AND GET IT ON THE BOOKS TODAY**. BABY STEPS TO BETTER HEALTH, AND IT'S ALL IN YOUR HANDS. NO ONE IS GONNA DO IT FOR YOU. GET IT DONE.

WHAT ATTRACTED YOU TO YOUR WIFE IN THE FIRST PLACE? THINK ABOUT IT THEN WRITE IT OUT BELOW.

WHAT 7 QUALITIES DO YOUR CHILDREN HAVE THAT CAN BE NURTURED? SOMETIMES IT'S BETTER TO FOCUS ON WHAT YOU CAN IMPROVE THAN WHAT YOU CAN ELIMINATE IN THEIR BEHAVIOR. NOT ALWAYS, BUT THE MORE ATTENTION YOU GIVE TO SOMETHING, THE MORE IT GROWS.

1.

2.

3.

4.

5.

6.

7.

HOLD HANDS WITH YOUR WIFE SOMETIME TODAY, AND DON'T LET GO FOR A WHILE.

WRITE YOUR WIFE A LETTER. GO TO A CRAFTS STORE, GET SOME OF THAT HEAVIER STOCK PAPER AND GRAB A NICE PEN WHILE YOU'RE THERE IF YOU DON'T HAVE ONE. REMEMBER WHY YOU FELL IN LOVE WITH HER, AND WRITE HER A LETTER TELLING HER HOW SHE MAKES YOU FEEL. TELL HER WHY YOU'RE ATTRACTED TO HER AND THAT YOU *APPRECIATE* HER. LIST ALL THE REASONS YOU CAN THINK OF, THEN FOLD IT UP AND LEAVE IT ON HER PILLOW FOR WHEN SHE GOES UP TO BED.

WHERE DO YOU SEE YOUR RELATIONSHIP WITH YOUR CHILDREN IN FIVE YEARS?
ARE YOU DEVELOPING RELATIONSHIPS THAT YOU'D WISHED YOU'D HAD WITH YOUR
PARENTS? ARE THEY LEARNING TO TRUST YOU AND BELIEVE IN YOU?

WHO ARE THE LAST 3 PEOPLE TO HELP YOU IN SOME WAY, MAJOR OR MINOR IN THE LAST FEW MONTHS? LIST TWO THINGS EACH YOU CAN DO FOR THEM SOON. IF YOU DON'T KNOW, ASK THEM. AND DO IT "JUST BECAUSE"

BUY A COFFEE AND BRING IT TO YOUR WIFE OR A FRIEND WHO NEEDS IT TODAY.

WHAT WORRIES ARE YOU HIDING FROM YOUR WIFE? CAN YOU SHARE SOME OF YOUR BURDENS WITH HER? WRITE THEM DOWN BELOW.

_____

_____

_____

_____

_____

_____

_____

_____

_____

_____

_____

_____

_____

_____

_____

WHO ARE YOUR FRIENDS? DO ANY OF THEM ANNOY YOUR WIFE? YOU DON'T HAVE TO GIVE THEM UP, BUT ASK YOURSELF WHY SHE DOESN'T LIKE THEM, AND TRY TO EMPATHIZE. DO YOU HAVE FEMALE FRIENDS SHE'S JEALOUS OF? MAKE A LIST BELOW AND ASK YOURSELF WHY SHE MAY HAVE A PROBLEM WITH THEM, AND HOW YOU CAN UNDERSTAND WHY SO YOU AREN'T DEFENSIVE (AND ARGUMENTATIVE) ABOUT IT NEXT TIME THEY COME UP.

1.

2.

3.

ANY MORE?

WHEN YOUR CHILDREN COME TO YOU WITH SOMETHING IMPORTANT, YOUR REACTION HELPS TO SHAPE HOW THEY SEE THE WORLD AROUND THEM. WHAT CAN YOU DO TO LISTEN BETTER, AND REACT IN A **POSITIVE WAY**? ESPECIALLY WHEN THEY'RE SCARED? <u>DON'T DISMISS YOUR CHILDREN'S FEELINGS.</u> IF IT'S IMPORTANT TO THEM, IT SHOULD BE IMPORTANT TO YOU. SHOW THEM BY HOW YOU REACT AND LISTEN.

WHAT ARE 3 THINGS YOU ADMIRE IN YOURSELF? WHAT HAVE YOU ACCOMPLISHED
THAT MAKES YOU PROUD, AND WHY?

1.

2.

3.

TELL YOUR LOVED ONES YOU LOVE THEM ON 5 SEPARATE OCCASIONS TODAY.

LOOK AROUND YOU. WHERE ARE YOU SITTING AS YOU READ THIS RIGHT NOW? AT HOME? IN A COFFEE SHOP? AT WORK?

WHEREVER YOU ARE, YOU'RE SURROUNDED BY BLESSINGS. CAN YOU SEE THEM? WRITE FIVE REASONS YOU HAVE TO FEEL THANKFUL RIGHT NOW, BASED ON THE THINGS YOU HEAR AND SEE AND HAVE GOING ON AROUND YOU.

SURPRISE **YOUR WIFE** BY HELPING OUT IN THE KITCHEN. CAN YOU MAKE DINNER BEFORE SHE GETS HOME? CAN YOU DO THE DISHES TODAY? BOTH?

WHAT DO YOUR KIDS REALLY LIKE TO DO? WHAT ARE THEIR INTERESTS? DO YOU SPEND TIME WITH THEM DOING THOSE THINGS? WRITE DOWN 3 THINGS YOUR KIDS ARE PASSIONATE ABOUT.

1.

2.

3.

BRING YOUR KIDS TO SEE THEIR GRANDPARENTS, UNCLES OR COUSINS. FAMILY IS IMPORTANT, AND **TIME WITH FAMILY IS IRREPLACEABLE.** IF YOU CAN'T DO IT TODAY, PICK UP THE PHONE AND SET A DATE WITHIN A WEEK. THEN TELL YOUR KIDS.

WHAT FICTION BOOKS HAVE YOU BEEN WANTING TO GET INTO? DO IT TODAY. GIVE YOURSELF PERMISSION TO PUT ASIDE WORK AND WORRY AND FIND SOME TIME FOR YOURSELF. YOUR MIND NEEDS A PLAYFUL REST.

MAKE YOUR WIFE BREAKFAST AND HAVE IT READY FOR HER WHEN SHE COMES DOWN. IF IT'S A WEEKEND, SERVE HER IN BED.

LIST TEN THINGS YOUR WIFE IS REALLY GOOD AT. LOOK OVER YOUR LIST AND
REFLECT ON EACH ONE FOR A MINUTE.

WHAT ARE 5 THINGS THAT MAKE YOU A GOOD DAD? THIS ISN'T THE TIME TO BE HUMBLE. WRITE THEM DOWN AND TAKE PRIDE IN YOURSELF. NOT EVERY DAD DOES THE SAME GOOD THINGS YOU DO. WHAT ARE YOU GOOD AT?

1.

2.

3.

4.

5.

WHAT ARE SOME UNREALISTIC EXPECTATIONS YOU HAVE OF YOUR WIFE? WRITE THEM OUT BELOW. START EACH
SENTENCE WITH, "I UNFAIRLY EXPECT...," THEN FINISH WITH, "BUT NOW I'LL..."

_____

_____

_____

_____

_____

_____

_____

_____

_____

_____

_____

_____

_____

_____

_____

WHAT CAN YOU BE PROACTIVE ABOUT TODAY THAT WILL POTENTIALLY SOLVE A PROBLEM YOU MAY BE FACING? IS THERE A LETTER YOU CAN WRITE? A CALL YOU CAN MAKE? THIS CAN BE HARD, BUT TRUE GROWTH COMES FROM WILING TO BE UNCOMFORTABLE TO MAKE THINGS HAPPEN.

UNPLUG FROM THE OUTSIDE WORLD. WHEN WORK IS DONE TODAY, LET IT GO. CLOSE YOUR LAPTOP, PUT YOUR PHONE ON SILENT AND PUT IT AWAY. RESOLVE TO STICK TO IT.

WHAT ARE 5 THINGS YOU LIKE ABOUT YOURSELF THAT YOUR WIFE APPRECIATES?
REALLY THINK ABOUT IT.

1.

2.

3.

4.

5.

DO YOU ANNOY YOUR KIDS BECAUSE "DAD" ALWAYS HAS TO BE RIGHT? WHAT ARGUMENTS CAN YOU **LET THEM WIN TODAY**, WHILE STILL BEING A GOOD PARENT, BUT LETTING GO OF YOUR STUBBORNNESS?

DESCRIBE THE THINGS YOU LOVE MOST ABOUT YOUR CHILDREN

WATCH A MOVIE YOUR WIFE WANTS
TO WATCH AND DON'T COMPLAIN.

WHAT IS THE ONE THING YOU'D BRAG ABOUT YOURSELF TO A STRANGER IF THEY ASKED? IS IT TRUE? IS IT ACCURATE? CAN YOU CREATE MORE OF IT?

WHAT DO YOU DO THAT ANNOYS YOUR KIDS? **DO YOU CRITICIZE THEM?** THE WAY THEY EAT, OR PLAY OR SOUNDS THEY MAKE? WHAT WILL YOU START DOING TODAY TO LET THESE THINGS GO?

WHAT'S YOUR IDEA OF A PERFECT WEEKEND IF YOU COULD HAVE IT ALL TO YOURSELVES?

RUB YOUR WIFE'S FEET FOR FIFTEEN MINUTES.
SHE'LL THANK YOU.

AND DO IT AT THE END OF THE DAY.

WHAT ARE YOUR KID'S DREAMS? DO YOU NURTURE THEM? OR DOWNPLAY THEM?
WHAT CAN YOU DO TO SUPPORT WHAT MATTERS MOST TO YOUR CHILDREN,
STARTING TODAY WITH SOMETHING SPECIFIC? WRITE IT DOWN BELOW...

WHAT DO YOU WISH YOU WOULD HAVE ACCOMPLISHED BY NOW THAT YOU HAVEN'T? FIND ONE, ATTAINABLE GOAL (WITH HARD WORK) THAT YOU CAN BEGIN WITH BABY STEPS TODAY. WRITE IT DOWN, MAKE IT HAPPEN. TODAY.

GIVE MONEY TO CHARITY.

RIGHT NOW, OR AT LEAST TODAY. IT DOESN'T EVEN HAVE TO BE A LOT. $5, OR EVEN LESS IF YOU NEED TO.

DONATE TO A REPUTABLE CHARITY AND MAKE THE WORLD A BETTER PLACE. HOWEVER, IN THE ACT OF GIVING, YOU MAY FIND YOU FEEL BETTER ABOUT YOURSELF, AS THE GIVER ALMOST ALWAYS BENEFITS MORE IN MANY WAYS TOO.

BE KIND TO YOUR WIFE ALL DAY NO MATTER WHAT.

EVEN IF YOU'RE HAVING A BAD DAY, RESOLVE TO FAKE IF NECESSARY, AND SOON IT WILL BE GENUINE. LET THE DOG OUT FIRST, PUT THE KID THINGS AWAY YOURSELF. GO BACK DOWNSTAIRS IF YOU'RE ALREADY IN BED AND SHE FORGOT SOMETHING, WANTS A DRINK OR WHATEVER IT MAY BE. BE KIND FOR NO OTHER REASON THAN THAT YOU LOVE HER, ALL DAY.

PLAN YOUR DREAM VACATION WITH YOUR WIFE. WHAT WOULD YOU DO? WHERE WOULD YOU GO? CAN YOU MAKE IT HAPPEN IN 5 YEARS? SKETCH OUT OR WRITE YOUR IDEAS BELOW...

WHAT ARE 3 THINGS YOU LOVE ABOUT YOUR KIDS? WRITE THEM BELOW, THEN SPEND FIVE MINUTES WITH EYES CLOSED CONTEMPLATING EACH OF THEM. IMMERSE YOURSELF IN THEM AND **THEN HUG THEM WHEN YOU SEE THEM NEXT** AND TELL THEM WHY THEY MATTER TO YOU. YOU'LL NEVER REGRET IT. **EVER.**

SCHEDULE 3 DAYS THIS WEEK AND COMMIT YOURSELF TO EXERCISING. CIRCLE THE DAYS AND WRITE WHAT YOU'LL DO NEXT TO THEM, **DON'T SKIP OUT**. HEALTHY HABITS START SMALL.

SUNDAY:

MONDAY:

TUESDAY:

WEDNESDAY:

THURSDAY:

FRIDAY:

SATURDAY:

HOW OFTEN ARE YOU MORE INTERESTED IN THE NEWS OR YOUR PHONE THAN YOUR KIDS?
RESOLVE TO DO IT DIFFERENTLY, STARTING WITH JUST TODAY. ONE DAY.

THEN SEE IF YOU CAN CONSCIOUSLY DO IT TWO MORE DAYS THIS WEEK. WHERE YOU
REALLY PAY ATTENTION TO THEM. NOTICE WHAT IT DOES FOR THEM AND
RESOLVE TO MAKE A LITTLE MORE TIME EACH WEEK A HABIT.

What are 5 Things you can do for your wife Today?

1.

2.

3.

4.

5.

Now...
Get,
Them,
Done!

MAKE PAPER AIRPLANES WITH YOUR KIDS AND HAVE A CONTEST TO SEE WHO'S CAN GO FARTHER. TEACH THEM TO MAKE ONE IF THEY DON'T KNOW HOW.

SURPRISE YOUR KIDS WITH A BOOK. READING IS SO IMPORTANT. IF THEY CAN'T READ, EVEN BETTER. DAD CAN NOW HAVE STORY-TIME. GO TO THE STORE AND GRAB SOMETHING NEW YOU'VE SEEN THEM EXCITED ABOUT. AND TELL THEM IT'S "JUST BECAUSE"

WHERE DO YOU SEE YOURSELF IN FIVE YEARS? IS IT GOOD? IF NOT, WHY? IF YES HOW DID YOU GET THERE? WHAT CHOICES ARE YOU MAKING TODAY THAT CAN DRASTICALLY ALTER THE NEXT FIVE YEARS AND GET YOU THE SUCCESS YOU WANT FOR YOURSELF AND FAMILY?

WHAT ARE SOME UNREALISTIC EXPECTATIONS YOU HAVE OF YOUR KIDS? WRITE THEM OUT BELOW. START EACH SENTENCE WITH, "I UNFAIRLY EXPECT...," THEN FINISH WITH, "BUT NOW I'LL..."

(THEY'LL NOTICE THE CHANGE AND LOVE YOU MORE FOR IT!)

WHAT ARE 3 THINGS YOU FIND SEXY ABOUT YOUR WIFE? HER CURVES? INTELLECT? HER SMILE? WRITE THEM BELOW, THEN SPEND FIVE MINUTES WITH EYES CLOSED CONTEMPLATING EACH OF THEM. IMMERSE YOURSELF IN THEM AND THEN AFTER, CALL OR AND TELL HER WHAT THEY ARE.

1.

2.

3.

...NOW GO TELL HER

PLAY ANY GAME FOR 20 MINUTES WITH YOUR KIDS. **HERE ARE THE RULES**: YOU MUST USE MORE IMAGINATION THAN YOU USE PROPS. PLAY MONSTER, HIDE-AND-SEEK, OR ANYTHING THAT DELIGHTS YOUR CHILDREN.

TURN THE TV OFF FOR ONE DAY. **YOU DON'T NEED IT.**

JUST ONE DAY, AND SEE HOW YOUR WORLD CHANGES.

THEN REPLACE THAT TIME WITH SOMETHING LIKE A **GOOD NOVEL** OR TIME WITH YOUR FAMILY.

DO YOU OFTEN ANTAGONIZE YOUR KIDS BECAUSE OF THE MOOD YOU'RE IN? WHAT
1-2 TINGS CAN YOU PUT IN PLACE TO REMIND YOURSELF NOT TO DO THEM AGAIN?
KIDS TAKE THEIR CUES FROM YOU... SHOW THEM YOU LOVE THEM INSTEAD OF
TAKING OUT YOUR STRESS ON THEM.

1.

2.

GOT MORE? BE HONEST AND KEEP WRITING, THEN COMMIT TO TAKING YOUR
STRESS PRIVATE...

TAKE YOUR WIFE ON A DATE TONIGHT, TO A PLACE SHE'D LIKE TO GO, BUT YOU HAVEN'T BEEN TO IN A WHILE. WRITE YOUR PLANS BELOW... HOW WILL YOU MAKE HER FEEL? WHAT WILL YOU WEAR? WHAT WILL YOU SAY TO MAKE HER FEEL SPECIAL TONIGHT? MAKE YOUR PLANS BELOW...

LIST TEN THINGS YOUR KIDS ARE REALLY GOOD AT. LOOK OVER YOUR LIST AND REFLECT ON EACH ONE FOR A MINUTE.

_____

_____

_____

_____

_____

_____

_____

_____

_____

_____

_____

_____

_____

_____

_____

FORGIVE YOURSELF FOR "THAT THING" YOU PUNISH YOURSELF
HARD FOR WHENEVER YOU THINK ABOUT IT.

FORGIVE AND KNOW THAT OTHERS HAVE DONE IT TOO, MADE THE SAME MISTAKE,
AND THAT YOU DON'T NEED TO CARRY THAT AROUND ANYMORE. IT'S TIME TO MOVE
ON. SAY, "I DID THAT, AND THAT'S OKAY. I'LL DO MY BEST TO NOT LET IT HAPPEN
AGAIN, BUT HERE'S HOW I'LL HANDLE IT IF IT DOES" AND MEAN IT.

WHAT ARE SOME UNREALISTIC EXPECTATIONS YOU HAVE OF YOURSELF? WRITE OUT AT LEAST 4 BELOW. START EACH SENTENCE WITH, "I UNFAIRLY EXPECT...," THEN FINISH WITH, "BUT NOW I'LL UNDERSTAND THAT I..."

1.

2.

3.

4.

WHAT IF YOU KNEW **YOU MIGHT LOSE YOUR WIFE** THIS WEEK TO TRAGEDY? WE DON'T LIKE TO THINK ABOUT THINGS LIKE THIS, BUT WHAT WOULD YOU TELL HER IF YOU BOTH KNEW YOUR TIME WAS LIMITED? WRITE IT OUT BELOW...

THEN GO TELL HER.

WHAT DO YOU DO THAT ANNOYS YOUR WIFE?

WHY DO YOU THINK YOU DO IT? CAN YOU MAKE CONSCIOUS EFFORTS TO WORK ON IT? ANSWER BELOW...

DO your children's homework WITH THEM, and don't rush just because you want to watch something or play on your phone. HELP THEM LEARN AND ENJOY IT, they grow up fast.

LIST 10 THINGS YOU'RE GRATEFUL FOR RIGHT NOW. THINK ABOUT THEM FOR FIVE MINUTES AFTERWARD AND SOAK IT IN. IT WILL CHANGE YOUR DAY. LIST THEM BELOW. THEN, MAKE A HABIT OF REVISITING THAT LIST AND EVEN FINDING NEW THINGS EVERY DAY TO BE GRATEFUL FOR.

WHAT ANNOYS YOU ABOUT YOUR WIFE? HOW CAN YOU LET IT GO BY WORKING ON YOURSELF INSTEAD OF TRYING TO CORRECT HER? ANSWER BELOW_

WHAT CAN YOU DO TODAY TO PUT A SMILE ON YOUR CHILD'S FACE? CAN YOU DO IT FIVE TIMES TODAY? GO FOR FIVE, BIG SMILES THROUGHOUT THEIR DAY, AND NOT ALL AT ONCE. COUNT 'EM UP!

WHO ARE YOUR FRIENDS? ARE THEY A NEGATIVE INFLUENCE? DO YOU REALLY NEED THEM IN YOUR LIFE? JUST BECAUSE YOU *FEEL* LIKE YOU OWE SOMEONE A FRIENDSHIP DOESN'T MEAN YOU DO. CULL OUT THE RELATIONSHIPS THAT HOLD YOU BACK. THINK ABOUT WHO THESE PEOPLE ARE IN YOUR LIFE, THEN PLAN TO MAKE A REASONABLE, HUMBLE EXIT.

WHO ARE YOU HOLDING A GRUDGE AGAINST? THEY MAY NOT EVEN KNOW IT, BUT THEY'RE GETTING TO YOU WITHOUT YOUR PERMISSION. CHOOSE TO LET IT GO. TODAY.

SURPRISE YOUR WIFE WITH A NECK OR BACK RUB **AND DON'T EXPECT ANYTHING IN RETURN** JUST DO IT BECAUSE YOU LOVE HER. TODAY. YOU DON'T HAVE TO DO IT EVERY DAY (ALTHOUGH SHE'D LOVE THAT). JUST SURPRISE HER.

WHAT ARE 3 SPECIAL THINGS YOU CAN DO FOR YOUR CHILDREN TODAY?

1.

2.

3.

WHAT CAN YOU FORGIVE YOUR WIFE FOR TODAY? LIST WAYS YOU'VE FELT HURT IN THE PAST (RIGHT OR NOT) AND FORGIVE HER FOR EACH.

1.

2.

3.

4.

MORE?

DO YOU LOOK AT YOUR CHILDREN WHEN YOU TALK TO THEM? EYE-TO-EYE? THEY NOTICE, TRUST ME. WHEN YOU SEE THEM TODAY, FOCUS ON THEM AND WHAT THEY'RE SHARING WITH YOU.

WHERE DO YOU SEE YOUR RELATIONSHIP WITH YOUR WIFE IN FIVE YEARS? HOW CAN YOU MAKE IT BETTER?

GO **SPLURGE ON SOMETHING FUN** AND LITTLE. DRIVE TO THE STORE AND BUY **THAT BOOK, MAGAZINE** OR **SHIRT** YOU'VE BEEN WANTING BUT COULDN'T JUSTIFY.

IT'S GOOD TO GIVE OURSELVES PERMISSION EVERY NOW AND THEN. LITTLE PLEASURES MAKE A DIFFERENCE...

ASK YOUR WIFE HOW'S SHE DOING. AT THE END OF THE DAY, ASK HER ABOUT HER WORK. THEN NOD AND LISTEN WITHOUT OFFERING ADVICE. SHOW HER THAT YOU CARE BY LETTING HER TALK.

TAKE YOUR KIDS OUT FOR ICE CREAM FOR NO REASON OTHER THAN THEY'LL LOVE IT.

(PSSST..... YOU WILL TOO..)

COLOR SOMETHING IN HERE WITH YOUR KIDS. TELL THEM IT'S YOUR SPECIAL BOOK
AND YOU'D LIKE THEM TO BE A PART OF IT.
LET THEM START IT.

GET YOUR WIFE A CARD FOR NO REASON, OR BETTER YET, **MAKE ONE FOR HER** YOURSELF TELLING HER **WHY SHE'S SO** SPECIAL.

LET YOUR KIDS SNUGGLE YOU FOR **TWENTY MINUTES** TODAY. <u>TIME WITH DAD IS PRECIOUS.</u>

DRAW OF PICTURE OF YOU AND YOUR WIFE HOLDING HANDS. THE MORE "INARTISTIC" YOU ARE, THE BETTER. THEN SHOW HER AND YOU CAN BOTH LAUGH.

NOW DRAW OF PICTURE OF YOUR KIDS BELOW.

THE GOOFIER THE BETTER.

CALL, SEND AN EMAIL OR **WRITE A LETTER OF APPRECIATION** TO SOMEONE OR SOMEPLACE THAT DESERVES IT. WE USUALLY DO SO WHEN WE HAVE SOMETHING TO COMPLAIN ABOUT. BE THE PERSON THAT BRINGS A LITTLE MORE LIGHT TO THE WORLD AND SHOW YOUR APPRECIATION RIGHT NOW.

YOUR JOURNEY HAS JUST BEGUN. IF YOU'VE DONE ONE OF THESE A DAY, OR AT LEAST A FEW A WEEK, YOU KNOW EXACTLY HOW EVERYTHING HAS IMPROVED, I DON'T HAVE TO TELL YOU.

AND CONGRATULATIONS...

(IF YOU HAVEN'T, IT'S NEVER TOO LATE TO START)

NOW GO, MAKE A DIFFERENCE, THE WORLD DESERVES YOU

Made in the USA
Coppell, TX
13 February 2021